Rich Board,
Poor Board

by

Caryl Hallberg

ISBN: 1511402806
ISBN-13: 978-1511402804

This Book Supports and is Dedicated to CARD

COLLABORATING
AGENCIES
RESPONDING TO
DISASTERS

The leadership at CARD believe that working together, we can mobilize our assets to create a better, safer, happier, more unified, more prosperous world.

Their role in making this a reality is to empower our community, groups, organizations, and individuals to respond to any emergency. The most important part of their work is their relationships.

CARD hopes their relationships, like all great friendships, include being there for you when you need them, supporting your goals, nurturing laughter and humor, respect, fun, and a long-term commitment to your well-being and happiness.

Together we build friendships, create community, and work toward a better world for everyone.

If you are like the vast majority of people, you resist thinking about negative things that might happen. The idea of you or your loved ones being present when a disaster occurs is terrifying. If you are reading this, and you live in a disaster-prone region but haven't embraced an empowered approach to readiness, please help us change how preparedness is shared in our communities - for all of us, but especially for those persons served by nonprofits and governmental agencies.

Persons served by nonprofits and agencies are some of

the populations that CARD targets with their message of fear-free and culturally appropriate emergency preparedness. CARD works primarily with nonprofits that serve low-income and special-needs communities.

In context, these targeted populations include members of our communities with little or no ability to address their own mitigation, preparedness, response and recovery efforts. CARD also targets people who might be socioeconomically challenged; those isolated by geography, gender, age, disability status, and risk status related to sex and gender, who may be considered. These groups are most frequently considered vulnerable or "at-risk populations" and have more recently been labeled in government efforts as people with "access and functional needs" or AFN.

In 1989, following the Loma Prieta earthquake, CARD was formed by a group of nonprofit agencies concerned with the needs of their clients, perceived as the most vulnerable populations in our communities. CARD was created to fill a gap that widens as the national conversation moves further toward aggressive, fear-based messages. CARD's mission is about partnership, between the many traditional disaster relief agencies and the thousands of nonprofits whose preparedness needs are inherently different from those of traditional disaster agencies.

CARD has developed an alternative curriculum and fear-free approach to fit the realities, abilities, and budgets of service providers whose consumers have access and functional needs, as well as other barriers to embracing traditional preparedness and response efforts.

When was the last time that fear motivated you to do anything for the long term? If you are like most people, fear may make you do something once, maybe twice. But once the fear subsides, it's back to the status quo. It is actually hope and maintaining a positive view that pulls or pushes you to do things over and over again.

Research shows these doom-and-gloom messages have NEVER worked. CARD offers something quite different -

it offers participants the opportunity to free their inner MacGyver, to use the resources we have all around us, and to actually leverage the incredible strength found in diversity, service, and community.

CARD supports the Alameda County Office of Homeland Security and Emergency Services to help ensure that vulnerable and underserved communities across the county have ongoing access to culturally appropriate emergency preparedness and disaster response tools, training, and support. In addition, CARD is the coordinating body and single point-of-contact for the nonprofit and faith-based sectors in the Alameda County Emergency Operations Center.

A primary way CARD complements traditional disaster response agencies is by providing easy, culturally appropriate, emergency service tools and programs, all designed for communities that need a more tailored, place-based approach. With a growing realization that many communities cannot and will not be reached by traditional disaster methods and agencies, many stakeholder agencies work with CARD to help build their capacity to serve diverse communities.

Frail seniors, children, people with disabilities, the homeless, Limited English Proficient (LEP) residents, medically fragile individuals, low-income families, and many others depend on their trained and trusted nonprofit agencies for critical services before, during, and after a disaster.

Trained, committed and united, local agencies are the best support for people with special needs in times of disaster.

CardCanHelp.org

CONTENTS

ACKNOWLEDGMENTS

Ana-Marie Jones, Executive Director CARD
An inspiration and gift to everyone she meets.

Photos by Ambro

Art by Mablema

Editor: V. Lord

PREFACE

Nonprofit organizations have Boards of Directors. The fact is that the success and commitment of the Board assures the success and commitment of the organization and its programs. If your Board of Directors is a Poor Board, your organization will be poor regardless of the effectiveness of your programs, administration, or executive commitment.

Rich Board, Poor Board is not about financial issues precisely; it is about effectiveness. Our definition of a Rich Board is one that is rich in resources of all kinds helpful to your organization's mission and goals. A Poor Board is one that is lacking in these resources. The intention of this booklet is to provide a quick guide to building your organization's Board of Directors into a Rich Board, one that will provide the stewardship, commitment, and growth you want for your organization.

Building a Rich Board is a tough job, but it is achievable for any organization. This booklet is a guide, but you must take the steps to create the outcomes. We will not be discussing insurance, legal, or tax issues within this context and recommend you consult with the appropriate professional on each of these issues as it relates to your Board of Directors.

The layout of this booklet defines Boards of Directors

and the ideal profile of a Board, then we move on to look at your specific Board of Directors and the pieces you should in have in place for your Board. Finally you will learn how to recruit prospective Board members and efficiently make them part of your governing body.

If you find what we have offered helpful, we would appreciate your letting us know.

Caryl Hallberg

1

WHAT IS A BOARD OF DIRECTORS?

*Boards are part of the tripartite
governance system for American
corporations:*

- Board

    - Boards control the organization and have the definitive authority in fulfilling the mission.

- Executive

    - The Executive serves at the discretion of the Board administrating the work of the organization

- Staff

    - Staff executes the work of the organization

These three parts are joined by the desire to achieve the mission of the organization. They must be gripped with a sense of purpose!

THE BOARD HAS THE TASKS OF:

- Fiduciary responsibility

- Stewardship

- Planning for the future

- Sharing the mission and translating it to the public

- Preparing policy

- Making contracts

- Influencing government

- Approaching donors

- Creating a collective institutional wisdom

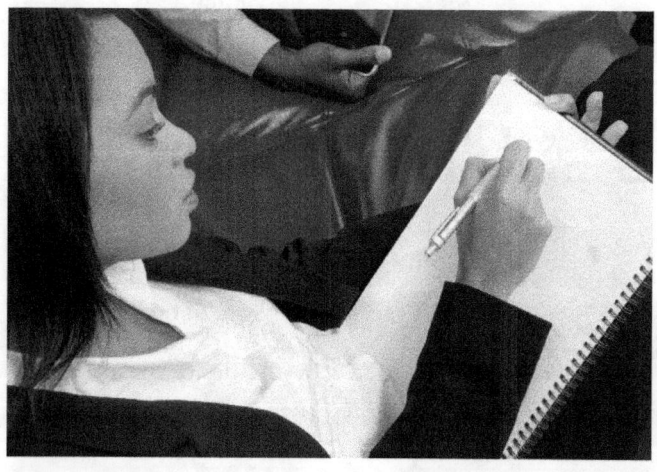

2

THE COMPOSITION OF THE BOARD OF DIRECTORS

An Ideal Mix

It is a good idea to assess the current members of your Board, or if you are just building a Board, the immediately available candidates for your new Board.

In general it is thought that an ideal working Board should be an 80/20 split:

80% influence and affluence

20% sweat equity

Tying the mission and goals of the organization to the backgrounds and personalities of the Board members will help create a committed Board, but you must approach this with an almost global view. It may make for a comfortable conversation if everyone on your Board is from the same social, interest, career field circles, but it reduces the Board's capacity to build awareness or create a diversity of thought when looking at tough questions for the organization. The more circles of influence present on your Board of Directors, the more people they can bring in to support the organization.

First look at the diversity of your current or immediately available Board members. Some of these may be more important to your Board than others. The point here is to think about it and become aware.

- Age

  - Youth brings energy to the table

  - Mid-life brings current business practices and influences

  - Seniors bring experience and sometimes wisdom

- Gender

- Culture or Race

- Location -

Depending on your organization it may make sense to have Board members who live in a broadly scattered geographic area or members who all live in a narrow geographic area like a single city.

- Experience -

Diversity of experience offers the chance for creative problem solving.

  - Past nonprofit Board experience

  - Nonprofit sector experience

  - New to the nonprofit sector

- Constituency and Clientele –

If your organization serves a special population, you may want to consider having one or two members who are citizens of that population on your Board.

- Affluence/Influence –

You want your Board members to have power to reach others who are important to your organization or to have access to wealth.

Persons who are able to reach others and have social influence are sometimes called connectors. Every Board needs connectors: these are the people who fill events and increase participation.

Persons who have access to money often, but not always, have wealth themselves. They are able to provide larger donations or have the ability to reach out to those who have that capacity.

- Social/society

- Government

- Business power centers

3

DEFINING THE ROLES OF BOARD MEMBERS AND OFFICERS

Creating a Board Agreement

Many organizations find it helpful to have a Board of Directors agreement that each new Board member signs as part of coming onto the Board. Think of it as a short job description for your Board members. These agreements outline in specific terms the basic requirements for participation on your Board. They may include:

- Attendance at some minimum percentage of all regularly scheduled Board meetings

- Attendance at the annual Board meeting

- Attendance at and/or participation in Fundraising events

- A specific Give/Get donation amount –

This particular responsibility is the most frequently discussed and most often balked at when considered, particularly by grassroots and start-up Board of Directors.

It is an important piece to the Board agreement, however, and can be critical to the success of the organization. Some institutional funders and some savvy individual donors will ask if 100% of the Board members donate to the organization. Think about it: if the leadership of an organization doesn't give to the organization, why should anyone else give?

A simple solution for more grassroots nonprofits is to simply have the Board members agree to annually give what is for that individual a "significant" or "stretch" donation.

- Give/Get –

This term relates to the idea that a person can simply *give* a cash donation from their own resources, or they can *get* a substantial cash donation from another source, say the corporation for which they work or a wealthy individual who respects their commitment.

- Participation on a minimum number of Standing or Ad Hoc committees

- Term of Board service

Much of what might be outlined in a Board Agreement will be defined in the organization's by-laws. When creating this one-page agreement always refer to those by-laws to remain consistent and assure that the Board of Directors is following the organizational rules.

4

CHARACTERISTICS NEEDED IN NEW BOARD MEMBERS

Assessing the Organizational Needs

This is a process that should be addressed by the Board Development committee briefly after each addition to the Board and thoroughly during any strategic planning sessions.

We have already looked at the issue of diversity. It is also important to consider personality when assessing characteristics you may want on your Board. Personality characteristics are fairly obvious to some degree in that we all want leadership, honesty, courage, commitment to service, and intelligence. You also should consider what sorts of characteristics will complement and enhance the personalities of your current Board members.

It is only when all the members convene at a Board meeting that your Board of Directors exists. You want them to fit together as a working whole.

Easier to nail down are the organizational needs around specialized professional skills. Expertise in these areas can make the process of setting policy and making decisions more effective and efficient for your Board. Some areas of special skills and attributes to consider are:

- Human resources

- Finance

- Public relations

- Fundraising

- Law

- Politics

- Medical

- Civil service

- Real-estate

- Marketing

- Social reach

- Commerce

- Investing

- Technology

- Access to key resources

■ Prior nonprofit Board leadership experience

■ Fame

This is by no means a complete list. Think about your organization and add those skills and attributes that may be missing from this list but key to your mission and organizational goals.

■ _____

■ _____

■ _____

■ _____

■ _____

■ _____

5

BUILDING THE BOARD

*Establishing or Refining the Process
for Assessing and Approving
Prospective Board Members*

It is key that you select Board members using a consistent process. You want your process to be considered seriously by current and prospective Board members. This beginning sets the stage for your Board members understanding and accepting the serious responsibility and the honor of serving on your organization's Board.

These are suggested steps once you have recruited an interested party for possible Board membership:

- Request they provide a resume or CV including all nonprofit and community service

- Ask for a personal reference from current or past Board member

- Alternatively, three personal references

  • preferably from the nonprofit sector

- Identify a clear fit with a current or near-future Board requirement

- Ask candidate to interview with Executive Director and one Board member

- Review of all gathered information done by Board Development committee, Nominating committee, or entire Board, whichever is most appropriate for your organization.

- Ask candidate for attendance at a minimum of one Board meeting

- Receive recommendation for nomination from committee membership, if that is appropriate for your organization

- Attain nomination for membership in the Board by a current Board member at an official Board of Directors meeting

  - The prospective member should not be present

- Attain second to the nomination by a current Board member at an official Board of Directors meeting

- Receive majority approval by the voting members of the Board according to organization's by-laws

- Offer invitation from the Board Chair or designee to join the Board of Directors

- Attain acceptance of the invitation within a preset amount of time

- Signing of Board agreement

- Send a welcoming letter from the Chair of the Board accompanied by a Board Manual.

6

FINDING PROSPECTIVE BOARD MEMBERS

Passivity Will Not Produce a Dynamic Rich Board

Finding new Board members can be a challenge, but now that you know for whom you are looking, it will be easier to focus on getting the best people for the job.

Finding Prospective Board members is an ongoing and active process. Your current Board members are your first line of prospecting. You may even want to make finding a new Board member part of their Board duties. Regardless, each Board member should be encouraged to find a new member for your Board before ending their own tenure on the Board.

You want to stay in an ongoing relationship with your Board Alumni, encouraging them to introduce possible Board candidates from their circles of influence.

Recommendations from current or past Board members bring the prospective Board candidate to the table with an immediate level of commitment you won't have from candidates acquired from different sources.

■   Informational Social -

A particularly productive way to build your Board is to ask your Board members and other lead volunteers to host small short informational gatherings for your organization.

These informal gatherings might be for 5 to 15 guests and can be located in a private home, at the organizational site, or any quite venue. Along with your host, the Board Chair and the Executive Director should be present. It is thoughtful to serve light snacks and appropriate beverages.

The event should contain a quick introduction of the key organizational persons present, an overview of the organization including its mission, vision, history and current program activities. If you have one, show a 10- to 15-minute video about your organization.

Have all of your collateral materials such as brochures, wish lists, donor pledge cards, etc. available on a table.

At the end of your presentation, have a short Q&A session and then allow the gathering to become social.

Do a good job of presenting your organization and the guests at the event will ask you what they can do to help.

You may not only generate a pool of potential Board members, you may also gain new donor support, new volunteers, or gifts of goods and services needed by your organization.

■   Organizational Website -

Your organizational website can be a strong selling point to potential Board members who will contact you after finding your website. Beyond the ability to access your services or make donations, be sure to have a way for interested people to effortlessly contact you regarding their interest. If you have openings on your Board, say so on your website and be specific about the attributes you hope to find. Update this page and consider its SEO.

■ Internet -

Speaking SEO, don't forget Internet search engines as a direct tool for finding the people you need to lead your organization. If you need a Board member who has an entertainment law background in Georgia, search on those criteria. As I wrote this I googled "entertainment law" Georgia and came up with more than 400 names of entertainment attorneys just in Atlanta, within the top four results. Without going much beyond three clicks out of Google, I found 14 possible candidates with an interest in nonprofit service, bios, and resumes including contact information. The entire process took three minutes. Do not overlook the possibilities that exist using this tool!

Social networks, particularly LinkedIn and Facebook, provide the ability to request introductions and referrals, along with the capacity to search specific characteristics or target advertising.

■ Philanthropic Institutions

- Your local United Way or community foundation may have a way of posting Board opportunities or listing individuals interested in finding Board opportunities. Contact them!

- Volunteer recruitment and training organizations often have a Board component to their services. To find a volunteer management organization suitable to your needs and location, do an internet search on "leadership opportunities" and "volunteer opportunities".

- Depending on where you are located, the 211 service for your area may have a means of posting the Board member openings or connecting you to persons looking for Board service.

- Explore any Leadership Institutes in your region to learn if they have a Board service development program or matching service.

■ Community Activities -

- The business and social sections of your local or regional newspaper offers daily insight into who the most affluent and influential are within your geographic area.

- Whenever possible, attend events that have as participants the types of people you want on your Board. Once there, talk to people you don't know, introduce yourself and your organization. Make it possible for the people you meet to contact you and be sure to ask them for an opportunity to contact them.

  - Fundraisers and informational gatherings for sister organizations are not the types of events we are suggesting. Allow your sister organization to have the focus be on them at these sorts of events.

- Join, attend, or offer to speak at civic organizations dedicated to community service and networking. If you have an immediate need for Board members, let it be known even if it means a small fine.

These are but a few of the ideas for finding potential Board members. Try sitting down with your Board Development committee and brainstorming additional ideas. All it takes is some thoughtful exploration and a desire to share the passion you have for your organization's mission and you will be able to find candidates to recruit for your Board of Directors.

7

RECRUITING PROSPECTIVE BOARD MEMBERS

You Are Interviewing Someone to Fill
an Important Job.

The subtleties of how the Board Development or Nominating committees arrive at deciding that a particular person is appropriate for your organization depends on too many factors to be discussed in this format. The key is to remember that an invitation to join your Board should never be hurried or treated lightly. You honor both your organization and the individual by following a formal procedure and treating the entire process seriously.

The Chair of the Board should issue an invitation to the prospective candidate, requesting an interview. When this interview is requested, the candidate should be informed of the purpose of the interview and offered any written public information available on the organization. If your organization has a media packet this is a fine tool to offer your candidate. This tool is particularly important if you do not have an up-to-date website or your website does not have a lot of meaty content. This strategy gives the candidate the chance to think about the idea and generate questions.

The interview is a business meeting and is best treated as such, though it is perfectly acceptable to suggest meeting over lunch or dinner. The Chair of the Board, as host, pays any tab of course!

The interview itself should be a clear presentation that includes:

- An overview of the organization

- Any problems it is currently facing

- General responsibilities and time commitments required as a Board member

- The very specific role the candidate will be asked to fill

- Why this candidate was chosen

You want your candidate to know that the selection committee has been thorough and diligent. It will increase the likelihood that your candidate will agree to serve your organization. If your candidate can respect the process, then that respect will transfer to the entire Board and the organization as a whole.

When you have a person who desires to be on your Board and has been the one to initially approach your organization instead of the other way around, do not be tempted to shortchange the organization or the individual. Take all the same steps of evaluating and recruiting this individual as you would with someone who you are approaching from outside your organization's sphere. A "yes" to a Board invitation should come from a base of respect, knowledge, and clear expectations.

People are flattered to be considered for a spot on your Board of Directors. Remember the worst that can happen when you identify a potential Board member and then ask for their interest is that they will say "no." Even if that occurs they will have learned more about your organization and may become strong supporters regardless of their agreement to serve on your Board; the candidate may even be able to suggest another person suited for Board membership.

8

THE NEW BOARD MEMBER

Formal Orientation to the Board and
the Organization

Materials a new Board member should receive can vary from organization to organization. In general the following should be part of the package:

- By-laws of the organization

- Media kit for the organization

- Strategic plan

- Most recent annual report

- Minutes from the prior 12-month period of Board activity

- Approved budget for current fiscal year

- Most recent financial statements accepted by the

Board of Directors

- Most recent audit report

- Copy of organizational policies set by the Board, particularly those policies governing paid and volunteer staff deportment:

  - Equality and diversity policies

  - Sexual harassment policies

  - Safety or preparedness policies

- Roster of Board of Directors members, with:

  - Contact information

  - Officer and committee roles of each member

  - Service terms of each member

- Schedule of next 12 months' Board meetings and other scheduled Board events

  - Date

  - Time

  - Location

Building Relationship Bonds

As soon as possible after full introduction to the Board of Directors, and possibly after their first attendance at a Board meeting as a voting member, the Chair invites the new member to a short meeting.

This is an opportunity for the Board Chair to build the relationship with this new Board member. It is a time to ask and answer any questions that may have come up through the review of the orientation materials.

It is also the ideal time for a conversation about committee membership of a role as a corporate officer of the organization.

If there are enough seasoned Board members, you can consider having a seasoned Board member act as an official mentor to a new Board member. This can relieve the Chair of having too many responsibilities and assures that each member of the Board has someone besides the Chair to whom they can turn with questions or concerns.

9

BOARD EDUCATION

Library

Every Board should build a small lending library for its members that can be read or consulted. The library should contain:

- Books general to Board development and management

- One copy of Robert's Rules of Order

- Books specific to the type of agency or organization the Board leads, written in general terms for the layperson

- Books specific to the types of services or the clientele the organization serves, written in general terms for the layperson

- Books on fundraising and philanthropy

- Subscriptions to and back issues of periodicals

33

pertaining to the general subject matter of Boards and nonprofit leadership and the specific areas of concern for the organization.

Training

A regular educational component is a healthy part of your Board meetings. The frequency of educational segments can be determined by the Board members during their annual planning session.

The educational segments of your Board meeting can be led by the Chair or a designee, a special guest of the Board, or by the Executive Director. These segments have endless topic possibilities. For example:

- Programs of organization

- How to understand financial reports

- Current trends in the nonprofit sector

- Trends or research related to the organization's area of concern, i.e. childhood development, medical breakthroughs, secondary education.

There are associations, collaboratives, and foundations serving the nonprofit sector that provide training opportunities and seminars specifically tailored to Board education. Make sure your Board has access to and knowledge of these opportunities. Encourage members to participate in these trainings according to their interests and then ask them to share what they learned with the other Board members.

If your Board has an annual retreat, this is a wonderful opportunity to insert an education component that is more in depth and targeted to an identified need for your Board.

Providing for Board education does more than simply foster a well-informed board. It builds the sense of a strong group dynamic; it revitalizes the energy of the individual members and the whole.

10

EVALUATING YOUR BOARD

Efficacy of Effort

How do you know how well you are doing as a Board of Directors? It is helpful to use an evaluative tool to measure your success and outcomes. I recommend you do one now and then again in six months, after having implemented the recommendations in this book.

Once you have established some norms and goals for your Board of Directors, an annual evaluation of the Board is useful in identifying what needs changing, updating, or renewal. Once actionable items are identified, the Board can set goals and assign SMART tasks and responsibility for completion of those tasks. This can be the Board's portion of the organization's strategic plan.

Questions to Ask

On a scale of one to five, with five being Rich and one being Poor, rate your Board in the following 12 areas:

- Our Board is made up of people who complement one another's talents and skills

- The structural composition of the Board is clear

- Our board is the right size to carry out all Board responsibilities and for deliberative action

- Our Board represents all the interests that should be consulted in forming policy

- There is an efficient working relationship between our Board, the Executive Director and Staff

- Our board understands the mission of our organization and how our programs achieve that mission

- Our board has a cohesive social rapport

- Our Board has formulated specific goals to guide its work

- Every member of our Board is involved and interested in the work of the organization

- Policy is set only after a clear deliberation and consideration

- Our Board has a sense of accomplishment

- Our Board maintains broad and effective relationships with the community

How did your Board of Directors do?
Do you have a Rich Board or a Poor Board?
Remember that all the steps and suggestions outlined in

this booklet are action steps; to get results, take action!

A Rich Board doesn't just build itself overnight. It takes time and perseverance. It takes strong leadership and a willingness to use your Executive Director as a consultant to the process. The commitment you bring as an individual to the prosperity of your organization will be reflected in the composition of its Board and the overall success of its programs.

Ultimately, the Richness of the Board is dependent on the richness of its individual members and their resolve.

ADDITIONAL READING

■ *Secrets of Successful Boards*
Carol Weisman, Editor
F.E. Robbins & Sons

■ *Nonprofit Boards: Roles, Responsibilities, and Performance*
Diane J. Duca
John Wiley & Sons

■ *Doing Good Better: How to Be an Effective Board Member of a Nonprofit Organization*
Edgar Stoesz, and Chester Raber
Good Books

■ *CarverGuide, Your Roles and Responsibilities as a Board Member*
John Carver, and Miriam Carver
Jossey-Bass

■ *Boards That Make a Difference: A New Design for Leadership in Nonprofit and Public Organizations*
John Carver
Jossey-Bass

- *Nonprofit Boards and Leadership: Cases on Governance, Change, and Board-Staff Dynamics*
  Miriam M. Wood
  Jossey-Bass

- *Welcome to the Board: Your Guide to Effective Participation*
  Fisher Howe
  Jossey-Bass

- *The Nonprofit Leadership Team: Building the Board Chair-Executive Director Partnership*
  Fisher Howe
  Jossey-Bass

- *The Essential Drucker: The Best of Sixty Years of Peter Drucker's Essential Writings on Management*
  Peter F. Drucker
  HarperBusiness

ABOUT THE AUTHOR

Caryl Hallberg is the author of the forthcoming book, *Navigating to Joy, 11 Steps to Making Your Dreams a Practical Reality*, and founder of DogWatch Navigation LLC.

Caryl has spent years helping businesses and Community Based Organizations (CBO) create strategic plans and collaborative efforts. She has provided leadership and training for dozens of large and small organizations.

Outside of a long association with the nonprofit sector and service to community, she brings focused leadership, marketing, planning, development, and management skills. Caryl has experience in outreach, public speaking, fundraising, event management, and the creation and empowerment of diverse communities in the nonprofit sector. She has participated in the development of volunteer programs and trainings, worked with news media as a spokesperson, built CBO collaboratives, and participated in the creation of UN Community Sustainability Papers.

Her interests have to do with children, family, health, agricultural sustainability, and higher levels of conscious living. She has herself been a single parent and has been challenged by several serious illnesses. Caryl discovered through these experiences that there are ways of viewing reality that are more productive and evolved than others.

She has decades of excellence in building enterprises and not-for-profit organizations into creative, effective resources. She is a proactive leader adept at creating vision and developing action plans to consistently drive donor revenues and maximize community awareness. She is an advocate who skillfully builds consensus to drive organizational growth and change, developing solutions to meet community needs and organizational challenges.

While she was managing partner of Fulfillment LLC, she developed strategic planning tools and trainings used to create highly positive outcomes for her clients. She has worked with many organizations in the San Francisco and Monterey Bay regions and across the USA, including the Volunteer Centers, United Way, and American Red Cross. These tools were transformed into a unique process that enables individuals to create their own personal strategic plan. Since 2004, Caryl has successfully guided artists, business professionals, retirees, new college graduates, and other persons in life-transition phases through her process of strategic life planning.

She serves on Boards of Directors and Advisory Boards for nonprofits in Connecticut and California.

ICF certification as an Executive Life Coach specializing in Emotional Intelligence and Group Coaching, Caryl Hallberg, through her company DogWatch Navigation LLC, now offers to work with you to not only discover where you want to go with your life but to specifically plan how to get there and achieve all of your dreams.

She works with individuals, formative groups, private-practice professionals, and small- to mid-size nonprofits offering project design, grant acquisition, strategic planning, internal policy and procedures consulting, and group or individual executive coaching.

DogWatchNavigation.com